PRAISE FOR

"Jon Zens is a master teacher for those who aren't afraid to think outside the box and esteem Scripture above human tradition. This book is more proof of Jon's ability to lead us back to God's original idea of leadership in the body of Christ."

— **Frank Viola**, author, speaker, blogger, frankviola.org

"No matter how the contemporary Church in America stumbles or disappoints us, it is a joy and a comfort to know there is someone like Jon out there teaching and preaching a biblical, Christ-centered way to be in the Body of Christ. Ekklesia, the ancient word used to describe the highly participatory, beautiful expression of Christ's Body on earth does not need more leaders. What the Church needs is her Lord and the love that emerges between brothers and sisters in Christ who take seriously the calling to be the church—a people who are eager to come to a place of maturity, fecundity, and fullness. The global pandemic left many empty seats in church buildings all across the nation, but also revealed a deep need among the church-going public for something more than a song and a sermon on Sunday mornings. The many pastors and leaders who are perplexed and crushed because of this would do well to read this book. *Don't Be Called Leaders* brings an antidote and answer to this problem providing the hope, help, healing needed to once again see the Church thrive."

— **Stephanie Bennett**, Ph.D., author of *Silence, Civility, and Sanity: Hope for Humanity in a Digital Age*

The lyrics used in chapter 7 by permission; from *Love Songs for Our Lord*, Gainesville, Florida, p. 36.

Copyright © 2023 by Jon Zens
First Edition

Cover art by Kristin Hollinger
Cover design by Rafael Polendo (polendo.net)
Interior layout by Matthew J. Distefano

PRINT ISBN 978-1-957007-79-3
ELECTRONIC ISBN 978-1-957007-80-9

This volume is printed on acid free paper and meets ANSI Z39.48 standards.
Printed in the United States of America

Published by Quoir
Chico, California
www.quoir.com

DON'T BE CALLED LEADERS

HOW LEADERSHIP HAS FRUSTRATED GOD'S ETERNAL PURPOSE

JON ZENS

"The words of the New Testament which the enthroned Christ has spoken through His inspired ministers of the New Covenant are His architectural directives for the holy task of constructing this new covenant home . . . The Old and New Testaments . . . will be seen as two separate and distinct architectural models for the house of God in two quite separate and distinct stages in history . . . This is to say that *the Old Testament is not the canon of the Christian church* . . . The form of government appointed in the old covenant is not community polity for the church of the new covenant . . . In these terms, the Old Testament, though possessing the general authority of all the Scriptures, does not possess for the church the more specific authority of canonicity. *Under the new covenant the Old Testament is not the current canon.*"

— Meredith Kline, *The Structure of Biblical Authority*, Eerdmans, 1972, pp. 85, 99, 102; emphasis mine

CONTENTS

I dedicate this book to Larry and Bev Lindseth, whose friendship, love and generosity have encouraged Dotty and I over many years!

WORDS OF THANKS

I would like to deeply thank Shelley Albert, Alison Hardy, Mary Ellen Robinson, and Charlene Wilder for their reading of this manuscript, and providing very helpful edits that improved the content.

FOREWORD

I write briefly in order to convince you to read Jon Zens' new book, *Don't Be Called Leaders*, from cover to cover, page after page, concentrating on paragraph after paragraph, one sentence at a time.

The Bible's concept of "church" is nothing like what you've experienced in your lifetime. *Don't Be Called Leaders* turns upside-down what it means for you to follow Jesus with His other disciples.

The Bible calls you and all of Christ's followers *the ekklesia*.

The translation of the Greek word *ekklesia* as "church" is unfortunate. When you read the English Bible and come across the word "church," you picture *"a building, a business, and a boss."* The word *ekklesia* simply and delightfully means *"a problem-solving community"* living out Christ's Life together. People who gather to address problems are *ekklesia*, whether the group of people follows Jesus the Messiah or Artemis. There's no leader among the *ekklesia* of Christ except for Yeshua, that is, Jesus the Anointed One (Christ).

This is the theme of Jon's book *Don't Be Called Leaders*. It might be called, *Don't Be Offended By Not Being Called a Leader*.

As a long-time traditional evangelical pastor, a President of the largest evangelical convention, and a candidate for United States Congress, I understand how people look to "leaders" to solve problems.

But in the *ekklesia* of Christ, there is no leader but Jesus.

"Do not be called leaders, for there is no leader among you but Christ" (Matthew 23:10).

Our Problem-Solver is Jesus Christ. He speaks and works through the *ekklesia*, not one man. Christians must understand the depth, diversity, and delight of the body of Jesus gathering to express His Life. The *ekklesia* is not a one-man show. It is a fountain of blessing from people who've met the Water of Life.

I've known Jon for years. I've learned from his writing ministry. *Don't Be Called Leaders* is a book I devoured in just a few hours. Jon walks us through his journey. He empowers us to comprehend the biblical concept of ekklesia. After reading *Don't Be Called Leaders*, you'll understand who the ekklesia are, and learn some implications for being the *ekklesia* in the world.

Wade Burleson
President, Istoria Ministries
Author, *Fraudulent Authority*

"Jesus has often seemed to be 'domesticated' in the Churches, turned almost into the representative of the religio-political systems, justifying everything in its dogma, worship and canon law: the invisible head of a very clearly visible ecclesiastical machinery, the guarantor of whatever has come into existence by way of belief, morals and discipline. What an enormous amount he has been made to authorize and sanction in Church and society in the course of Christendom's two thousand years! How Christian rulers and princes of the Church, Christian parties, classes, races have invoked him! For what odd ideas, laws, traditions, customs, measures he has had to take the blame! Against all varied attempts to domesticate him, therefore, it must be made clear: Jesus did not belong to the ecclesiastical and social establishment."

— Hans Kung, *On Being A Christian*, 1978, p. 177

1

CHRIST IS THE LORD'S MIND

My guess is that most church goers are not conscious that Jesus even uttered these words, "Don't be called leaders, for One is your Leader, the Christ." There is certainly little evidence that believers take seriously what Jesus said. In the context, Jesus' main point is that when people are elevated and venerated by the use of titles, the *preeminence and supremacy of Messiah is diminished and overshadowed*. "For One is your Teacher, and you are all brethren . . . for One is your Leader, the Christ."

Our Father sent the Son into the world, and set His seal upon Him (John 6:27). The delight of the Father is Jesus Christ. But here's the clincher: everything in heaven and earth, everything in the universe is at the service of the Lord's "eternal purpose which He made in Christ Jesus our Lord." This purpose is wrapped up in a mystery that is unveiled in the cross, by which Jew and Gentile are made "one new humanity," the *ekklesia*. *The Message* puts Ephesians 1:20-23 so powerfully: "All this energy issues from Christ: God raised him from death and set him on a throne in deep heaven, in charge of running the universe, everything from galaxies to governments, no name and no power exempt from his rule. And not just for the time being, but *forever*. He is in charge of it all, has the final word on everything. At the center of all this, Christ rules the *ekklesia*. The *ekklesia*, you see, is not peripheral to the world; the world is peripheral to the *ekklesia*. The *ekklesia* is Christ's body, in which he speaks and acts, by which he fills everything with his presence."

We can clearly see, then, that an issue like calling people "leaders" is diametrically opposed to God's eternal purpose in His Son to create a kingdom of equal brothers and sisters. A case can be made that the inordinate focus on leaders in church history has done more to stifle the expression of Jesus in His *ekklesia* than anything else. Just think of the unending list of books on leadership, such as John Maxwell's *The Leader's Greatest Return: Attracting, Developing and Multiplying Leaders* (Thomas Nelson, 2020).

The Lord's Jesus-purpose is to result in the *ekklesia* displaying to the heavenly realms *now* in history the many facets of His wisdom (Ephesians 3:10). It is thus imperative to have a revelation of what it means for Christ to be building His *ekklesia*.

2
WHAT IS EKKLESIA?

E *kklesia* is such a pivotal word, yet few have a clue what it entails. Christ rules the universe, yet His heart is set on one primary purpose: "I will build My *ekklesia*" (Matthew 16:19). We would do well, then, to know what Jesus is constructing.

Please put on your thinking caps for reading about *ekklesia*. It is hard to know where to start. There are so many layers of issues, but at the end of the day the tragedy is that most people's assumptions about "church" are false, and the truth is buried in the cemetery behind the church building.

"Church" is the English word used in most versions of the Bible to translate the Greek word *ekklesia*. For example, Jesus said, "I will build My *ekklesia* . . ." Most English Bibles render this, "I will build My church." The truth is, "church" is a terrible translation of *ekklesia*.

You can Google "church or ekklesia" and find out why "church" is manifestly inappropriate. But here is a concrete illustration of a serious problem. When Tyndale's English translation of the New Testament appeared in 1526, he correctly rendered *ekklesia* as "congregation" or "assembly." But on two occasions, Acts 14:13 and 19:37, he translated *ekklesia* as *churche* because it referred to pagan places of worship. Isn't that fascinating?

Out of the 115 times *ekklesia* occurs in the NT, the King James Version rendered it "church" 112 times. Three times, Acts 19:32, 39, 41, it translated it as "congregation," because a non-Christian gathering was in view. Isn't that interesting!

The word "church" should be purged from our vocabulary. It had its origins in paganism, communicates nothing authentic, masks the life of Christ in the body, and is usually visually connected to buildings that appear every half-mile in America. Yet this is the word embedded in people's minds when they think of "Christianity."

Authenticity is to be found in what the word *ekklesia* meant in Jesus' and Paul's day. Don't forget, Jesus said He is building "My *ekklesia*," not "My church." Jesus' disciples would have been familiar with this word in two ways.

First, it was used in the Greek translation of the Old Testament (called the *Septuagint*) to translate the Hebrew word *Qahal*. This referred to the Israelites *as assembled together*, often before the Lord.

Secondly, *ekklesia* was commonly used in the civil realm and had in view *a duly assembled group of citizens who came together to discuss and take care of common concerns in the community.*

Thus, this word primarily had both a spiritual and civil usage in the first century. Out of many choices, Jesus selected this word to define His building project. He used *ekklesia* three times in Matthew, once in chapter 16, and twice in chapter 18. In light of all the revealed dimensions, *ekklesia* must be defined as *the Lord's people gathered together to carry out the whole gamut of Christ's kingdom purposes.* In light of what *ekklesia* actually entails, we need to expand our horizons. We are used to thinking of "church" in terms of going to a building, sitting in pews, working our way through a bulletin, singing a few songs, hearing a sermon, shaking some hands and going home. But the NT expression of *ekklesia* involves much, much more—especially the dimension of being a problem-solving community.

Matthew 18:19 is often quoted at prayer meetings and appears on plaques in homes: "if two of you agree on earth concerning anything they ask, it will be done for them by My Father in heaven." The problem is, the crucial context is usually forgotten when this verse is cited. The setting is one where the saints are dealing with unrepentant sin. It is here that Christ used *ekklesia* twice. "And if he/she refuses to hear them, tell it to the *ekklesia*. But if he/she refuses even to hear the *ekklesia*, let him/her be to you like a heathen and a tax collector."

Matthew 18:15-20 shows that the saints comprise a problem-solving community. Notice that the *body* handles the issue. There is nothing in the passage about "the leaders" doing anything. The concern is brought to the *ekklesia*.

Paul's letter to the Corinthians also shows that the *ekklesia* is called upon to deal with a wide spectrum of thorny issues.

- The saints clustered around personalities; they were to repair the breach and be one-minded

- There was serious immorality going on; they were to gather together and take care of the problem

- There were disputes being taken to unbelieving judges; they were to resolve such matters among themselves

- There were inconsiderate, divisive actions taking place in their eating together; they were to wait for one another

- There were disruptions going on in their gathering; they were to let everything be done for the building up of one another

More could be listed, but you can see how Paul assumed that the saints could take care of difficult problems by the Spirit's help, instead of defaulting to specific leaders. Again, notice that Paul never directed any remarks specifically to "leaders." *He addressed the letter to the brothers and sisters.*

This is why I try to use the word "church" for what goes on in the religious world, and the word *congregation or assembly* for authentic *ekklesia*. You can see pretty obviously that the matters the early assemblies tackled are almost never touched by "churches." Have you ever heard of a local church helping to resolve disputes among its members—with or without the involvement of "leaders"?

Ekklesia is present when a body of Christ-followers is committed to Him and to one another to pursue all aspects of His kingdom, as we have pointed out in Matthew 18 and 1 Corinthians. You can do "church" without *ekklesia* being a reality. "Church" can be carried out without commitment to anything beyond going to a building, singing some songs, putting some money in the plate, and listening to a sermon.

In light of what we've seen entailed in *ekklesia*, a serious misconception needs to be corrected. I don't know how many times I've heard preachers/Bible teachers say, *"Ekklesia* means the people who are 'called out.'" I hope you can see that putting it like this totally takes the edge off of the word, and makes it innocuous. *Ekklesia* involves spiritual commitment with others to pursue the will of Christ. "Church" is something which, as R.C. Sproul confessed, you go to primarily to hear a sermon.

"Binding and loosing" was a function in the Jewish culture that only the Rabbis carried out. People would come to them with ethical dilemmas, and they would forbid ("bind") or allow ("loose") based on their understanding of the Law and the traditions of the elders. However, in Matthew 18:18 Christ grants this "binding/loosing" function to the *ekklesia* as they take care of kingdom business. That which was limited to the "clergy" of the Jewish religion, Jesus conferred on all His people as they gathered. This highlights again how the body of Christ is a Spirit-led, decision-making organism.

Our study of *ekklesia* also uncovers the fallacy of the idea that "church" consists of meeting with people for coffee occasionally. The functioning of *ekklesia* revealed in the NT involves a *group of believers in a locale.* For many believers in our culture right now, meeting from time to time with others for fellowship is all they have, but the NT concept of *ekklesia* is more robust than that. Paul could write a letter to an identifiable group of saints in a city. How could a problem be "taken to the *ekklesia"* if there is no group of believers committed to their Lord and each other? How could disputes be resolved by a few people who meet for coffee periodically? The NT assumed that believers were in ongoing relationships where the 58 one anothers would be meaningful (e.g., "comfort one another," "prefer one another," etc.).

Because the word "church" has so much incorrect baggage and human tradition attached to it, most people have become desensitized to the actual realities of our identity as Christ's *ekklesia.* We would do well, then, to consider this crisp summary of the word:

"We belong to a heavenly political system called the *Kingdom of God,* and we have a King called Jesus the Christ. We all are heavenly citizens of the '*ekklesia* of God' and we come together purposely to make Spirit-led judicial *policies* and *decisions* in light of the Kingdom of God on earth, that is, we participate in binding and loosing" (Skeeter Wilson, 2001, author of *Take Nothing With You*).

In light of what is really wrapped up in who we are as the *ekklesia*, all vestiges of "church" should be jettisoned. *Ekklesia* is the life of Christ flowing through the saints to carry out His purposes. There's a whole lot of "church" going on, but how much *ekklesia life* is really taking place?

3

MY JOURNEY FROM CHURCH TO EKKLESIA

B efore getting into the meat of my concerns, I thought it would be helpful to share some of the key moments when Jesus first revealed to me His *ekklesia*, His Bride. Our perspectives are formed as He brings any number of puzzle-pieces across our pathway. I have certainly been blessed over the years by the Lord sending brothers and sisters who have spoken Christ to me in love.

In 1966, I found Alexander Hay's *New Testament Order for Church & Missionary* (1947) in a South Carolina bookstore. As a student at Bob Jones University, I read it in my room whenever I was alone until it was completed. Looking back, it had some shortcomings, but it was on target in one crucial area: the traditional practice of each local church focusing on one pastor was not in the New Testament. So, by 1966 I had no interest in "the pastorate."

In 1975. we moved from Philadelphia to Nashville, Tennessee, to work with Norbert Ward, who in 1972 was the founding editor of *Baptist Reformation Review*. Norbert asked me to be Associate Editor in 1976. Somehow Ken Leary got a copy of BRR and contacted me. Ken was part of a three-family community living on a multi-acre parcel of land in Nashville. Ken asked to visit our little group that met in Norbert and Naomi's basement. Ken then suggested that we meet and study a book together. We started going through Louis Berkhof's *The History of Christian Doctrines*.

During our third session, Ken asked me a question based on his visit to our meeting in Norbert's home. "Jon, why do you stand in front of a podium and teach?" I was a bit offended by his query. I quickly responded with, "As Paul said, 'The Lord has ordained by the foolishness of preaching to save those who believe.'" But Ken came back with, "For sure, but 'preaching' in the New Testament was directed toward unbelievers, it was not central in the gathering of believers." Ken's words planted a seed in me that would blossom as time elapsed.

Then in 1978, Al Lewis and his family moved to Nashville from Wyoming to be part of our fellowship. Because of Norbert's health challenges, we were now meeting in a small rented storefront. After two months, Al asked if he could talk with me after our gathering one Sunday. He wondered why our get-together was basically a few songs and hearing me teach. He felt that we would be more blessed by having an open meeting along the lines revealed in 1 Corinthians 14. I assured him I would look into this and get back to him. In the following months, I researched this matter before the Lord, and revisited Ken Leary's remarks to me about "preaching."

After much wrestling, I tentatively concluded that both Ken and Al were right: the New Testament provided evidence neither of the "centrality of preaching" in body gatherings, nor of the structured "service" found in most church bulletins. In 1980, I ended up collating my thoughts into an article entitled "Building Up the Body: One Man or One Another?" Because the content was so controversial, this draft was sent to seventy-five respected brethren (many of them were pastors), and I asked for feedback before I would publish it in *BRR* in 1981. I received seven replies and felt their defense of sermons was anemic, and so the manuscript was published in the Summer, 1981, *BRR* (Vol. 10, #2). It was reprinted in my 2011 book, *The Pastor Has No Clothes*.

1977 was a game changing year for me. In February, I was invited to participate in an assembly, and speak to them over a long weekend. I was never the same after being in their midst. They began in 1972 with fifteen people, and when I came in 1977 there were 150. Most of them were new converts coming out of the hippie drug culture. The backbone of this ekklesia consisted of five home groups, and then on Sunday they rented a church building later in the day where everyone came together for teaching and fellowship. Three mature brothers taught the people how to study the Scriptures for themselves. The asking of questions in all settings was encouraged.

Before leaving on Monday, the three brothers met with me. They asked me to read Ephesians 2, Colossians 2, and Galatians 3. Next, a number of questions were directed to me concerning the Law in these passages. Then they asked if I had read *The Reformers and Their Stepchildren* by Leonard

Verduin. I told them I had this book but had not read it yet. They strongly encouraged me to read it.

I don't remember how, but I came across Howard Snyder's *The Problem of Wineskins* and I read it in early June, 1977. It took my understanding of *ekklesia* to a new level. Snyder showed how the early church was relational, simple, and was marked by caring for people both inside and outside the body of Christ. This explosive era had no buildings, no clergy, and no rituals. He contrasted this Christ-centered simplicity with the later developments of church structures, a hierarchy of church officials, and an increasing focus on religious rites and customs. When I put this book down, I was stunned. I felt like my "church" world was shaken to the bone.

But deeper shaking was coming. Later in June, I read *The Reformers and Their Stepchildren*. I was well-read in Calvin's and Luther's views of the church. I was always troubled by something in their writings, but I couldn't put my finger on it. For example, in one sermon Calvin addressed his audience with these words: "Some of you are drunkards and adulterers, and God's judgment is at your doorstep." I'm thinking, "How could he say such things and not confront them personally about such behavior?" And, "Why would such people be found in a church service?" Verduin's book opened up the answers to such important questions. Since the advent of Emperor Constantine around 325 AD, church was defined, not by belief in Christ, but by territory. When a child was born, it was baptized and thus viewed both as a citizen of the state and part of the church. In Catholic and Protestant cities the citizens were *required* to be in church, or they could be punished by fines or otherwise. People had no choice but to "go to church." This helped me understand why the Anabaptists were so hated by Catholics and Protestants. They opted for a believers' *ekklesia* and for believers' baptism. Leonard Verduin's numerous insights opened up many vistas for understanding the crucial things that went wrong in church history, and how *ekklesia* was buried under layers of human traditions.

4

OUR OBSESSION WITH ONE-PERSON MINISTRY

It is a deeply ingrained assumption that each local church needs a pastor. If a pastor dies or moves away, the search for a replacement kicks into gear, as is illustrated by Elizabeth Actameier's book, *So You're Looking for a New Preacher: A Guide for Pulpit Nominating Committees* (1991).

Why is the need for one leader so pervasive? Well, one large factor was the development of the office of bishop in the post-apostolic church. In Paul's day, the *ekklesias* had open meetings where all could participate, but later such gatherings faded and more and more attention was given to leaders. G. Wolfgang Forell pointed out this tragic shift.

> Yet the institution most effective in containing the threats to the nascent Christian movement was the gradually evolving *office of the bishop*. Ethical guidance for people recently converted to Christianity . . . was offered at first by a polyform ministry of grace, reflected in the New Testament. But as time went by moral authority was increasingly focused in an ordered ministry of bishops and deacons (*History of Christian Ethics*, Vol. 1, Augsburg, 1979, pp. 39-40).

So, originally Christ was speaking and working through the brothers and sisters as they ministered and cared for one another. This was an outworking of the Lord's eternal purpose for the *ekklesia*. But, as the bishop's authority increased, the functioning life of Jesus in the body receded.

Traditional views of church are always concerned to find a final seat of authority—in a bishop, in a pastor, in a church board, or in a congregation.

But this approach misses entirely the crucial reality that *Christ is the final authority*. The body of Christ meets under His leadership, and He expresses Himself through the brethren. *The buck stops with Jesus, not with any human(s) on the earth.*

Since the rise of one-bishop rule, around 200 A.D., a one-person orientation has dominated church leadership at all levels, and in all denominations. The essence of this practice is captured in a statement by Jan Paulsen, "The local church pastor is key—absolutely central—to everything we are and do as a church" (*Ministry*, July/August, 2010, p. 4). This conviction reflects the universal thinking, written or unwritten, about how churches are run.

Here are four examples of how strongly and dogmatically the one-person dependence is spelled out as "God's will."

> John Owen (1616-1683): ". . . on this office ['pastor'] and the discharge of it He hath laid the whole weight of *the order, rule, and edification of His church* (*True Nature of a Gospel Church*, abridged edition, p. 55).

> Frank Owen: "This fellowship, like a flock, needed a leader like a shepherd . . . An orderly church needs one overseer, one shepherd, one pastor . . . the pastor needs to have general oversight of the education, music, youth, activities and any other ministries of the flock . . . Allow this old veteran to observe that chaos easily develops where no one is in charge. If the church is to be one flock, it needs one shepherd . . . Wise church members will encourage this" ("The Pastor," *Western Recorder*, January 14, 1981, p. 11).

> David McKenna: "[The pastor] is like the cerebellum, the center for communicating messages, coordinating functions, and conducting responses between the head and body . . . The pastor is not only the authoritative communicator of the truth from the Head to the Body, but he is also the accurate communicator of the needs from the Body to the Head"

("The Ministry's Gordian Knot," *Leadership*, Winter, 1980, pp. 50-51).

C. Peter Wagner: "The army has only one Commander-in-Chief, Jesus Christ. The local church is like a company with one company commander, the pastor, who gets his orders from the Commander-in-Chief. The company commander has lieutenants and sergeants under him for consultation and implementation, but the final responsibility for decisions is that of the company commander, and he must answer to the Commander-in-Chief... The pastor has the power in a growing church . . . The pastor of a growing church may appear to outsiders as a dictator. But to the people of the church, his decisions are their decisions" (*Your Church Can Grow*, Regal, 1983, pp. 66, 67).

Such sentiments indeed are in line with the assumptions of most church leaders and church members. But they are dangerously out of touch with the Lord's eternal purpose in His Son to create by the cross a body of equals who together listen to and express the mind of their *sole* Leader, the Lord Jesus Christ. Paul unequivocally said, "the body is not one part, but many." The way churches function, based on the statements by Owen, McKenna. and Wagner, you would think the body is *dependent* and focused on one part, not many.

Our obsession with one-person leadership has nullified God's eternal purpose to have a Bride in which *all* can share their portion of the indwelling Christ. It can be said with solid basis, therefore, that "the pastor" tradition is an "obstacle to every-member functioning" (Frank Viola/George Barna, *Pagan Christianity?*, Tyndale, 2008, p. 105).

The Lord's eternal purpose in Christ is to display His multi-sided wisdom in this age through His *ekklesia*. The historical focus on one human leader is contradictory and destructive to His wisdom. His wisdom was spoken in the cloud of shekinah glory on the mountain: "This is my Beloved Son, listen to Him" (Luke 9:35). Truth be told, our ability to hear Jesus is crippled when we are taught by church leaders that our relationship with Christ must be mediated by the pastor who "is not only the authoritative communicator of the truth from the Head to the Body, but he is also the accurate communicator of the needs from the Body to the Head" (David McKenna).

It must be underscored that *any way of doing church that cultivates and fosters dependence on, focus on, deferring to, elevation of, and listening only to one leader (or plurality of leaders) is against and will thwart the Lord's purpose for His Son to be expressed through His Bride now on earth.*

Julia McMillan crisply puts into words how most leaders and people in the pews think:

> There is one primary voice in leadership. Where there is a pastor, that should be the only decisive voice that we hear. He is charged with soul care and is the ultimate voice the congregants expect to hear, especially regarding matters of vision and direction for the church (*Prophetic Crack: Pushers in the Pulpits, Addicts in the Pews*, 2010, p. 105).

There is so much detailed attention given to leaders that we have an article directed to them like this: "How to care for your voice: Eight practical suggestions for preachers" (Derek Morris, *Ministry*, July/August, 2010, p. 24).

Such ideas account for why we are so far from the *ekklesia* the Lord desires. We are not listening to the Son: "Don't be called leaders, for you have One Leader, the Christ, and you are all brothers and sisters."

5

THE CLERGY SYSTEM EATS UP THOSE IN ITS FOLD

B ecause the blatant, brazen, and pervasive practice of one-person ministry is so far from the Lord's mind, it is no surprise that hosts of men, women, and children are deeply damaged by their tenure in it. At this time, the average pastorate lasts just over two years. "It's lonely at the top of any organization," said a 1998 bulletin of Denver Seminary. In 2016, John L. Thomas wrote, "burnout in the first three to five years has become so prevalent" (*Encounter*, 76:1, p. 68). One pastor confessed, "On the surface it looks like I have dozens of friends, but the truth is that I'm the loneliest man in town" (Aubrey Malphurs, "You Can Count On Me," *Moody Monthly*). The effects of attaching the notion of divinity to the Pharaohs was noted by Barrows Dunham, "He became remote as gods are, unapproachable except by a few consecrated persons, mostly of his own family. A stifling etiquette surrounded him. He knew, in dreadful perfection, the loneliness with which power curses the powerful" (*Heroes & Heretics: A Social History of Dissent*, Alfred A. Knopf, 1964, p. 7). As Henri Nouwen observed, "The paradox indeed is that those who want to be there for 'everyone' find themselves often unable to be close to anyone" (*The Wounded Healer*, 1972).

Max Lucado observed, "We all lug loads we were never intended to carry" (*Traveling Light*, 2001). Pastors wear many hats and carry out numerous duties that the Lord never intended for one person to bear. Is it any wonder that so many collapse under burdens imposed by a job description nowhere to be found in the Lord's heart?

I am not going to supply a list of statistics that reveal how much damage has been done by the one-person leadership model. But here are two that should break our hearts: "The majority of pastors' spouses surveyed said that the most destructive event occurring in their marriage and family was the day the pastor entered the ministry . . . 80% of adult children of pastors surveyed have had to seek professional help for depression" (The data was collected by Richard A. Murphy; cited by Ivan C. Blake, "Pastor for Life," *Ministry*, July/August, 2010, p. 6).

The clergy-centered magazine, *Men of Action*, freely admitted, "Pastors are worn out, discouraged, and in need of affirmation. In fact, poll after poll reveals that most pastors are battling isolation, depression and loneliness. They are so beaten up by the ministry" (November, 1995, p. 4).

The history of the pastoral institution reveals a trail of devastation, burnout, broken families, mental illness, and suicide. The list of church leaders who have gone astray morally and financially is miles long (see The Roys Report, JulieRoys.com for a detailed sampling of pastoral failures). And what most often happens to those who fall? They go through various sorts of restorative rehabilitation and are sent back into the very same system that brought about their downfall. That's the definition of insanity: doing the same thing over and over and expecting a different result.

But here's the real point to be made: *the whole system that showcases one-person primacy is corrupt to the core.* The essence of its agenda puts Christ on the periphery and exalts those behind pulpits. This system fulfills Christ's words: when you look to and depend on leaders, the leadership of Christ is minimized, or possibly eliminated. So how can we expect good fruit from a method that has no roots in the Lord's mind?

We have built a hydra-headed infrastructure without any revelation from the Lord Jesus. Look at all the books, conferences, and seminars on pastoral leadership, better preaching, church administration, training leaders, and church growth. They are all pretty much built around the one-person model, which cannot be found in the New Testament (anywhere).

Roman Catholic theologian, Hans Kung, freely admitted that the bulk of religious traditions are not of divine origin.

> Those who so far have not been seriously confronted with the facts of history will sometimes be shocked at how human the course of events was everywhere, indeed how many of the institutions and constitutions of the church—especially the

Roman Catholic institution of the Papacy—are man-made
(*The Catholic Church: A Short History*, p. xxv)

In light of so many human traditions being turned into laws, Kung asks,
"Is it possible to imagine Jesus of Nazareth at a Papal mass in St. Peter's,
Rome?" (*The Catholic Church*, p. 6).

Are we willing to admit that the long-standing practice of one-person
leadership is strictly a *human tradition*, not having any foundation in the
New Covenant revelation? And yet we have put all our eggs in the one-leader
basket, and we have built church buildings and ministries around this false
assumption. Are we concerned that the one-leader idea has hindered the
ekklesia's true mission in Father's eternal purpose?

Jack Deere gives a great illustration that we can use to think about
"church." "If you were to lock a brand-new Christian in a room with a Bible
and tell him to study what the Scripture has to say about healing and miracles,
he would never come out of the room a cessationist" [a person who believes
that certain Spirit-gifts ceased with the closing of the New Testament canon]
(*Surprised by the Power of the Spirit*, Zondervan, 1993, p. 54). I would reframe
Jack's illustration like this: if you were to lock a brand-new Christian in a
room with a New Testament and tell him to study all it says about *ekklesia*,
would he ever come out of the room with any revelation about one person
being the key to church-life, and who would preach a sermon every Sunday
morning? Yet we have constructed our key notions about church upon a
foundation that is nowhere to be found in the New Testament. Isn't this
cause for alarm and re-evaluation?

We have in place a system centering on the leadership of one person. This
way of doing church has hurt both the leaders and those in the pews because
it is not the Lord's heart—it is not in line with His eternal purpose in Christ.
Are we going to continue the insanity of doing religious things over and over,
expecting a different result, or are we going to wake up and stop focusing on
leaders and pursue our true Leader, Christ?

6

POWER OR RELATIONSHIPS?

W e are told on the right hand and the left that each local church must be guided by a pastor. Yet there is zero information about this alleged need in the New Testament. What is in the New Testament are 58 "one anothers" that describe a vibrant body-life flowing out of the *ekklesia* in each locale. As was noted earlier, when the leader-bishop grew in power and prominence, then body-life was forced into the background. Leaders squelched Christ's life coming out of the body, and thus dimmed the light of His eternal purpose.

An underlying issue in church history is the matter of *power*. Obviously, there is a Spirit-power that Jesus gives to His people that goes out to help and serve others. But there is also the reality of fleshly religious power that seeks to control and dominate people. With the shift from body-life to bishop-control, fleshly power ascended, and as a result the bulk of church history is about power-plays by leaders to rule churches and territories. The power of Christ to serve others was marginalized. Henri Nouwen put his finger on how fleshly power deflected Christianity away from God's eternal purpose in His Son:

> Power offers an easy substitute for the hard task of love. It seems easier to be God than to love God, easier to control people than to love people, easier to own life than to love life. Jesus asks, "Do you love me?" We ask, "Can we sit at your right hand and your left hand in your Kingdom?" . . . The long painful history of the church is the history of people ever and again tempted to choose power over love, control over

the cross, being a leader over being led . . . One thing is clear to me: The temptation of power is greatest when intimacy is feared. Much Christian leadership is exercised by people who do not know how to develop healthy, intimate relationships and have opted for power and control instead. Many Christian empire builders have been people unable to give and receive love (*In the Name of Jesus: Reflections on Christian Leadership*, Crossroad Pub., 2002, pp. 77-79).

We have to face the fact that the story of the visible church is marked by the desires of church leaders to keep congregants under their thumbs. The real tragedy is that the one-leader system engenders the movement to fleshly power. The New Testament is about *relationships*, the 58 "one another's," beginning with the new commandment, "love one another as I have loved you [on the cross]." Again, as Nouwen observed, "The temptation of power is greatest when intimacy is feared. Much Christian leadership is exercised by people who do not know how to develop healthy, intimate relationships and have opted for power and control instead." The one-leader paradigm is essentially non-relational, and then they are taught in seminary not to be chummy with the congregation, and to keep their distance from the flock.

The Lord's eternal purpose in the first century saw face-to-face, relational communities spring up wherever the Gospel was proclaimed. The one-person fixation that came later brought with it patterns that turned life-bearing communities into lifeless institutions, often led by power-hungry leaders.

We would do well to remember the power of our Lord Jesus Christ's example of being low to the ground, looking up.

> In the foot-washing, the Lord humbles himself not only to the level of the disciples, but lower, beneath them. If the Lord wants to remove all disgrace from humans, he must place himself in a position in which one need not look up to him, but can look down to him. In this lower position that he adopts, he courts us, earnestly and urgently, and not just in passing. So low does he place himself that none of the lofty or the lowly

can feel themselves passed by. The Lord in his humility will always stand lower than any other human being (Adrienne von Speyr, *The Farewell Discourses: Meditations on John 13-17* [1948], Ignatius Press, 1987, p. 18).

The one-person power paradigm muddied the Lord's eternal purpose to conquer and win hearts by the power of humility as manifested in Christ.

It is imperative that we see the picture in the Tabernacle. One could not enter the tent of meeting without first going to the brazen altar, which symbolizes the cross, and then the washing laver. When the priest approached this laver it was a sea of glass, not one molecule of water was above another. After washing their hands and feet in this laver, they were prepared to enter the tent of meeting. The Kingdom of God is like a sea of glass, a body of equals: "you are all brothers and sisters," said our Lord.

7

WHERE IS THE PULPIT IN 1 CORINTHIANS 14?

T he shift from body-life to bishop-centeredness impacted how believers
came together. The early church met in such a way (usually in houses)
that all could share the living waters of Christ flowing out of them: "each one
of you has a song, a teaching . . ." But as time elapsed the meetings became
"church services" in which leaders were prominent. Ultimately, the "homily,"
or sermon, of the leader became the center point of getting together. The
historical development of the weekly sermon is well-documented in David
C. Norrington's *To Preach or Not to Preach? The Church's Urgent Question*
[SPCK, 1996], (Ekklesia Press, 2013, 214pp.).

As mentioned earlier, the early church was *relational*, and this was reflect-
ed in their open, participatory gatherings. "Change takes place when truth
is presented in relationship . . . To be healthy, a church must present truth
in the context of encouraging relationships" (Larry Crabb/Dan Allender,
Encouragement: The Key to Caring, Zondervan, 1984, pp. 84, 91).

It must be underscored that these open gatherings were centered on
Christ: "where two or three are gathered in my Name, I am in their midst."
Christ is *in* His people by the Spirit, resulting in living waters flowing from
their innermost being. When we come together He must be the end all be
all of our time together. We must echo and pursue Paul's passion wherever
he traveled: "For I am determined not to know anything among you except
Jesus Christ and Him as crucified."

Closely entwined with these thoughts is what drove Paul as he got up each
morning, having had stones thrown at him, or whatever, the day before: "for
the love of Christ constrains me, having concluded this, that one died for all ...
so that those who live would no longer live for themselves, but for Him who
died and rose on their behalf" (2 Cor. 5:14-15). A passion for Jesus brought

the believers together and held them together. If their love for Him faded—if they lost their first love—then a vacuum would come to be filled by things other than Christ. This is exactly what occurred as history moved on: organic love for Christ grew cold, and the resulting vacuum was filled by institutional leaders.

First century scholars from all quarters acknowledge that what began on the Day of Pentecost was a home-based movement. In a review of a commentary on 1-2 Timothy, the author said, "The historical and archaeological background is also put to effective use, as in his observation that 'Christians did not build churches until after the Edict of Toleration in 313 C.E.' and that earlier Christian assemblies were held in private homes that were only later enlarged and remodeled, such as Peter's house in Capernaum and the house church in Dura Europos" (*Ministry*, July/August, 2010, p. 60).

The eventual centrality of the leader's sermon was unknown during the early days of the *ekklesia*. The ascendancy of the sermon nullified the free expression of Christ through His gathered people. Gone were the times when unbelievers came into an open meeting, experienced everyone prophesying, and fell down on their faces and acknowledged that the Lord was in their midst. As David Valeta observed years ago:

> In many churches today preaching is given too much importance. Preaching has become the center of the church service, and this is detrimental for two reasons. First, monologue communication where one person speaks and everyone else listens is limited in its effectiveness . . . Secondly, I can find no support from the Scriptures for structuring church services around preaching by one person. Instead, 1 Cor. 14 indicates a meeting where participation by all believers is encouraged ("The Perils of Preaching," Bethany Theological Seminary paper, ca. 1979).

Why don't we align ourselves with the Lord's purpose to have open gatherings where Jesus can be expressed in innumerable ways? Why do we continue to perpetuate a method of meeting that shuts down the body and focuses on a leader, for which there is no basis in the New Testament? Again, being leader-centric runs counter to the Lord's purpose for His Son to be expressed by all the saints. Why don't we have assemblies where we can loudly, joyously sing:

> We're here to have a feast today
> Hurrah! Hurrah!
> We're here to eat and drink of Christ
> Hurrah! Hurrah!
> We're going to open up our mouths
> And let the living Christ come out
> And we'll all be satisfied
> By the Lord in His House
> For we know each member
> Has a portion of this Christ
> Hurrah! Hurrah!
> And when we come together, we'll
> Display, display
> The depths and riches of this Christ
> The newness which is in His life
> And we'll all be built up
> Into the house of God

(Tune: When Johnny Comes Marching Home)

It would seem that many leaders are afraid of 1 Cor. 14 because an open time would threaten their control. As Leonard J. Coppes said, "much of what happens in our worship services is standardized" by "ordained eldership" (*Are Five Points Enough? The Ten Points of Calvinism*, Reformation Educational Foundation, 1980, p. 179).

In any event, way back in 1898 David Thomas uncovered insight about the meeting in 1 Cor. 14:

Is the Christian church justified in confining its attention to the *ministry of one person*? In most modern congregations there are some Christian people who by natural ability, experiential knowledge and inspiration, are far more qualified to instruct and confront the people than their professional and stated minister. Surely official preaching has no authority, either in Scripture, reason, or experience, and it must come to an end sooner or later (*The Pulpit Commentary: I Corinthians*, F.W. Farrar & David Thomas, Funk & Wagnalls, pp. 429-433).

I Cor. 14 is an important part of New Covenant revelation. It is our largest window to see how assemblies functioned. For the most part, when people go to church Sunday mornings, usually around 11a.m., the service spelled out for them in the bulletin has no resemblance to the "each one of you," and "you may all prophesy one by one," in 1 Cor. 14. We claim to "go by the Book," yet the way we traditionally assemble has nothing to do with Christ's revelation about fellowship. We've let a leader-led paradigm snuff out the expression of Christ among the brethren.

Again, if you put a new believer in a room with a New Testament to read over and over, she would never come out of the room proclaiming, "Preaching is the divinely appointed means of blessing; preaching is the main means by which the people of God are built up in faith; it is through the preaching of the Word that the people of God will grow in their knowledge of God" (H.M. Carson, *Hallelujah! Christian Worship*, Evangelical Press, 1980, pp. 27, 71, 72). What H.M. Carson said is not the Lord's mind at all, yet his ideas permeate what structures most church services. Do we care that we are ignoring, avoiding and nullifying God's voice in 1 Cor. 14 in order to carry out a leader-centered human tradition? Do we see the vast blessing the evil one is keeping us from by deflecting us from eating and drinking of Christ together?

To illustrate how embedded the sermon/pulpit is in our practice, Jim Anderson said in *Unmasked*, "Does He mandate leaders to emphasize the importance of purity a full 20 percent of the time? If that were the case, 10 out of 52 sermons a year would be" on this topic (Lifeline Ministries, 2012, p. 89).

Where does the Lord mandate anyone to deliver 52 sermons a year? What in the New Testament would lead us to believe that church is structured around a weekly homily by the pastor?

The Lord's eternal purpose in His son desires for the *ekklesia* as a body to be a conduit to display the many-faceted wisdom of God. Because of our fixation on leaders, we block this display as many ears listen to a mouth, instead of many parts listening to the Son and sharing the treasures of His wisdom.

8
WHAT DOES ALL OF THIS MEAN?

The basic contours of what I've shared seem to be based on historical facts and New Testament perspectives. If my basic points are accurate, then the questions emerge, "What do we need to re-visit?" and "What are we going to do?" Following is a bullet points list to facilitate our thought/heart processes.

- Are you beginning to see that the *ekklesia* is central in His eternal purpose in Christ? "For the purpose that *now* to the principalities and powers in heavenly places through the *ekklesia* the many-faceted wisdom of God might be made known" (Ephesians 3:10). The Day of Pentecost was a coming of Christ by the Spirit to His *ekklesia*. "I will come to you," Jesus announced, and from that day forward the body of Christ was to continue and carry on the ministry of Christ on earth. The *ekklesia* is not an afterthought, it is in the forefront of His thoughts and purposes for His Son.

When have you ever heard a preacher/Bible-teacher express how vital it is to see everything flowing out of God's eternal purpose in Christ? You just don't hear it, and that accounts for why His revealed purpose in the Son is so muddied by the leader-centered way we do things.

- In light of the richness of the word *ekklesia*, we must realize how deceived we are in thinking that just because a religious building has a marquis out front that says "First Baptist Church," does not mean that *ekklesia* is actually happening in the group. Given what *ekklesia* involves—commitment to others to live out Christ's life and will together—we are left to conclude that there is very little of it taking place in most "churches."

- The early church met with Christ in simplicity in homes, and ate meals together. Think about it: all religions had a specific place (a synagogue, a temple, a shrine, a building) where they were to go and do their religious rituals. The first believers in Jerusalem and beyond had no inclination to erect structures to meet in: they gathered in homes around Jesus. Should we not re-visit the inordinate emphasis on buildings that we have inherited? It is interesting to note that with the increased focus on church buildings came the dependence on and multiplication of leaders. Can you appreciate how the Spirit-led life of Christ in the body was rendered irrelevant as "church" became more institutional and dominated by leaders? Do Dietrich Bonhoeffer's words have any resonance in our hearts? "The Church is the Church only when it exists for others. To make a start, it should give away all its property to those in need."

- As we have seen, the gathering portrayed in 1 Cor. 14 was robust, Spirit-led and open to the contributions of all present. In a word, it was *supernatural*. What is supernatural about most traditional church services, where people in pews stand up and sit down as they work their way through an order of service? Why does 1 Cor. 14 have no place in our practice? What reason do we have to believe that the Lord is excited about us singing some songs, putting some money in a plate, hearing a sermon, shaking a few hands and going home to a roast in the oven? Did Jesus die a wretched death to insure that we could look at the back of people's heads in the pew in front of us? Reflect on the untold blessings of Jesus we are missing by hearing a sermon by one person, instead of taking in a symphony of Christ from many voices.

- In the New Testament preaching Christ was an activity directed to unbelievers, often outdoors. There was no pulpit or preacher present in 1 Cor. 14. Later in history, what took place on the streets and marketplaces was brought inside the believers' gatherings. The speeches of leaders then became the center point, and the "each one of you has" dimension died out. There is no revelation in the New Testament about the "centrality of preaching." Rather, the Father's purpose is for the saints to express Christ together. The evil one has brought in the one-leader orientation to squelch the voice of Christ in the body. Are we ready to rise up and challenge the voice of one in order to restore the beautiful voices of many? How long will we allow the sermon of one to drown out the symphony of Jesus in the assembly?

- All of us have a propensity, like Israel, to want a king, somebody that will tell us what to do. But we need to understand that this feeling is from below, not above. In any configuration of believers, if there emerges a practice of assuming that one, or a few, will direct the meeting, choose the songs, and do the teaching, the battle has already been lost. The passion of any group should be to see the Lord Jesus lead them each time they meet. Big churches usually place trained leaders in their home groups to make sure things stay in line with their goals. Often, they will discuss the pastor's recent sermon in the small groups. But God's ideal is to have an open atmosphere where the Lord Jesus' leadership can direct and speak through each member. We are so used to leader-dependence that it is hard for a group to ask Him to lead and trust Him to supply. But if you ask, He will not give a stone or a scorpion, but His satisfying presence.

- There is ample evidence that most people choose the church they will attend based on their assessment of the pastor. This is a bogus way to come to a conclusion since there is absolutely nothing in the New Testament about "the pastor," as we conceive of him/her. Have you ever considered how much the leader-focus contributes to division among Christians? In Paul's day people were clustering around personalities – "I'm of Paul," "I am of Peter," and "I am of Apollos." Paul spent a lot of time rebuking such sinful immaturity. But the one-leader scheme is in lock step with encouraging people to identify with an apparent successful preacher. Let's face it, most churches are built around the personality of the leader. "People start coming to hear that one guy (most often it's a guy). . . . a personality people come to hear as if the proclamation of the gospel is some form of entertainment or consumption" (David Fitch, "Sayonara, Senior Pastor," Out of Ur, February 19, 2007). Attachment to leader-personalities ultimately contributes to more division among believers. Once again, when leaders are exalted, unity in Him is significantly challenged.

- I would like to address the following comments and questions to pastors and church leaders.

There is nothing in the New Testament to substantiate the common notion that the local church pastor is the key to all that we do in church. Further, there is nothing in the New Testament that reveals the office of "the pastor" as traditionally practiced.

You are in a position that the Lord does not recognize. Your livelihood depends on filling a position that is unknown in the New Testament. You spend a lot of time constructing sermons, sometimes staying up late on Saturday night to finish them. But sermons are not anything the Lord cares about. He's not going to judge how good and polished your sermons were. And your Lord Jesus said, "Don't be called leaders, for you have One Leader, Christ."

Does it concern you that the leader position you hold is blocking the full, free expression of Christ in the assembly? You claim to go by the Bible, yet you will come up empty trying to find "the pastor" in its pages. How can you justify going on in a profession that is based on air and tradition, not substance? Would you be willing to step back and just function as a brother/sister in the assembly?

The whole infrastructure (how-to books for clergy, books on preaching, seminaries, ministerial associations, leaders' conferences, rehab for burnout, seminars for pastors' wives) built on top of "the pastor" is a house of cards. How can you go on pretending that this charade is how you should invest the rest of your life? I'm convinced that most pastors go to bed at night knowing that there is something deeply wrong with the church system they are in, that what goes on in it does not cultivate authenticity, and too often the way church is run is about as spiritual as a rock in the desert. Henri Nouwen pinpoints a problem that plagues professional ministers:

> Christian leadership is a dead-end street when nothing new is expected, when everything sounds familiar and when ministry has regressed to the level of routine. Many have walked into that dead-end street and found themselves imprisoned to a life where all the words were already spoken, all events had already taken place, and all the people had already been met (*The Wounded Healer*, 1972).

This whole leadership trip has been a logjam in the Lord's purpose for almost 2000 years. Are you ready to quit perpetuating that which bears no resemblance to Christ's mind? Are you feeling a desire to repent from being part of a clergy system that opposes Christ's kingdom at every turn? "Not so among you, for you are brothers and sisters": a sea of glass, not a hierarchical pecking order.

You claim to go by the Bible for beliefs and practices, but if you were locked in a room and read the New Testament repeatedly, you'd never find the leader-centered, leader-dependent system you are in. Would this give you reason to pause and consider withdrawing from a methodology unknown to the Lord?

Perhaps you are pushing back with, "Yes, but hasn't He has blessed sermons to the salvation and encouragement of myriads of people for hundreds of years?" This response is purely *pragmatic* and misses the real issue at hand: *if our desire is to be led by the New Testament, where is the pastor/sermon/pew model in its pages?*

- These words and questions are directed to those non-leaders sitting in the pews.

Most of you for numerous years have gone to church buildings and heard hundreds of sermons. You probably have never heard teachings from 1 Cor. 14 because the chasm between what Paul wrote and what churches practice is too embarrassing. So, you have been devoting your time, energy and money to doing church in a way that has almost nothing to do with the purposes of the Lord in His son. You are complicit in allowing a leader-dominated practice of church to go on unabated.

Are you willing to say enough is enough, and lovingly challenge the pastor/pulpit centrality? There is nothing in the New Testament about it, and it is like the emperor having no clothes. Untold damage has been done by sacrificing the many voices of Christ in the assembly to hear one voice coming from a pulpit. Isn't it time to put your foot down and affirm that this perversion of God's purposes must stop?

Why do we say things like, "Good morning, pastor Joe," or, "Pastor is coming over for dinner tonight"; but we don't say, "Hi, teacher Sally," or, "Good to see you plumber Harry"? This way of speaking about leaders is a huge red flag that the sea of glass is being violated.

Each and every believer has, as Jan Vanier put it so beautifully, "a deep well inside of them. If that well is tapped, springs of life and of tenderness flow forth. It has to be revealed to each person that these waters are there and that they can rise up from each one of us and flow over people, giving them life and a new hope" (*From Brokenness to Community*). The prominence of leaders for centuries has kept these deep wells from expressing Christ. Are you feeling the need to repent of your silence and move toward the full expression of Jesus in His body?

There is an amazing picture in Genesis 26:15-22 that deals with wells. Abraham (picture of Christ) had dug some wells with living water. Envious Philistines in Isaac's time filled these wells with dirt. Isaac (another picture of Christ) re-dug these wells and gave them the same names Abraham had given them. Perhaps we can draw a broad parallel: Christ opened up the wells of living water on the Day of Pentecost, but by 200 AD these wells were filled with leaders. The time is beyond ready to have the leaders step aside and let the wells of Christ flow once again.

- The Lord is very grieved about the dominance of leaders and the resulting passivity of those in the pews. We know the Lord evaluates what goes on in assemblies, as described in Revelation 1:20-3:22. To five of the seven *ekklesias*, Christ issued the command to *repent*, or else He would remove His presence from them.

If what I have presented in the preceding bullet points has captured the essence of Christ's mind—"Do not be like the Gentiles . . . for you are all brothers and sisters"—don't leaders and those in the audience need to repent and return to their first love? Leaders should repent because they have blocked His living water for too long; those in the pews should repent because they have let the blocked wells go on without challenge.

What are you as a leader and you as a pew-sitter going to do with the fact that what we do as "church" has no roots in the Lord's heart? Are we willing to dig new wells where Christ's living water can flow freely? The Lord's *ekklesia*-purpose in His Son is at stake. Are you willing to remove yourself as an impediment blocking the living water of Christ?

If you are complacent and nonchalant regarding the seriousness of leaders blocking the living water, you do well to remember that there is a mighty shaking coming, and it has already begun.

9

THE SHAKING

By George Dunn

M y good friend, George Dunn (who passed in February, 2022) wrote these sobering words in February, 2019. I read this essay at his memorial service in April, 2022, in North Carolina.

Many years ago the word of the Lord came to me and I was told to prepare because, "Everything that can be shaken will be shaken." Everything? Yes, everything! Over the past twenty years I have watched this great shaking by God. Countries, governments, political systems, religious systems, economic systems, educational systems, and even Christian institutions have and are being shaken. There is a tremendous earthquake in the Spirit. However, the reason for this shaking is *not* punishment! It is not judgment! It is sent to test and to reveal the nature and quality of what has been built up. This shaking will reveal what is temporal and what is eternal and cannot be shaken! It reveals not only the inferiority of the building materials used but also the inferiority of human workmanship.

As this shaking intensifies in the days to come, all not built upon the Rock will crumble and fall. Only that built upon the sure foundation of the Lordship of Jesus Christ will remain. Only His reign and His kingdom are eternal.

I prophesy to you today that soon there will be much wailing in the land as all the things of this world in which we have placed our faith and trust begin to fall and come to ruin.

Hopefully, this shaking will bring people to cry out for something real—for something more trustworthy—something that can withstand the shaking and the coming onslaught of events and pernicious evil! That desperation, I believe, is soon to be experienced by those who up til now seem at ease, self-satisfied and even smug! Yes many who call themselves Christians will soon discover that their religious house is built upon the shifting sands of human reason, tradition, ease and comfort, pleasure, sensuality, personal preference, and human leaders.

One would hope that this shaking will affect the leaders who are clogging up the wells of living water. We have been fed the line for years that the key to better churches is to train more leaders. Many sources have trained a host of leaders over the years, and leaders have dominated the religious scene since our country's inception, yet there is no evidence that the status quo has changed to any significant degree. Has the life of Christ yet burst forth in His body on earth as a result of the proliferation of leaders?

10

EVADING THE LORD BY SERMONS AND PEWS

In 1966, Clyde Reid wrote *The God-Evaders: How Churches & Their Members Frustrate the Genuine Experience of Christ* (Harper & Row, 118pp.). I believe his perspectives need no commentary. We pooh-pooh what he said fifty-seven years ago at our own peril. Ask the Lord what course He wants you to take in light of Clyde's insights.

> The presence of God is not limited to the institutional structures, and to reject the institutional churches is not the same as rejecting God or rejecting the Christian faith.
>
> "Churchy" thinking is one of the great heresies of the modern church—the notion that unless one appears regularly in a certain kind of building labeled a Christian church, God has no relationship with them whatsoever. This is a manifestation of the current "preacher-cult" in which the clergy emphasize church attendance as the heart of the religious life, and thereby maintain a Sunday morning fan club. Some people may have to reject the churches to find Christ and vitality, for there are many churches where it is almost impossible to find or to recover that vitality. And God is surely present outside the churches—often more present without than within. God's Spirit is free in the world, and not captive in the churches. The Spirit of God has always resisted our efforts to put Him in a box and control our access to Him. The Spirit moves where He will, and sometimes it has to bypass the comfortable,

respectable structures we call religious, and speak to us in fresh ways and unaccustomed tongues.

[It is a mistake to identify] the *ekklesia* with the churches. It is not simply a matter of frailty. I believe the evidence is now overwhelming that we are dealing not alone with simple imperfection, but with a basic flaw or flaws in the way the churches are structured. The churches are suffering not from a minor infection, but from a serious malignancy which requires radical surgery rather than first-aid measures.

We structure our churches and maintain them so as to shield us from God and to protect us from the genuine expression of Christ.

We structure the services of worship as to prevent genuine worship. We use the clergy as buffers to protect us from the direct impact of religious influence.

Basically, we do not want anything to happen on Sunday morning that will upset our daily routine. We want to be "inspired," to come away with a warm feeling, but we do not want to be disturbed. So subconsciously we structure the service in order to assure safe, predictable, comfortable results.

I am absolutely convinced that the Bible is used as a tool for the avoidance of God's message to people today.

We employ clergy in such a way that they become buffers between us and God, religious professionals who fulfill our Christian duties for us.

The over-all picture is bleak. The need for drastic change in the very structure of our congregations is desperately urgent! We must upset the comfortable balance imposed by our ambivalence, and move from evasion to repentance to action, or our churches will slowly wither into relics of a bygone era.

[One] possibility is being tried by groups here and there. It is to withdraw from existing institutional structures for the purpose of becoming free to create a new and more flexible structure for a particular mission in the world.

It is apparent that time is running out for the churches as they presently exist. They must change or perish. A revolution is called for within the ranks of the organized churches . . . It might even call for an end to the paid ministry eventually. If this is where the Spirit leads us, let it be so. At least we will have regained our integrity and our honor as a Christian fellowship.

[We need] more emphasis on smaller, functioning units in which every person knows every other person by first name and mutual caring becomes possible.

The required action now is for us to want to change badly enough that we are willing to face with radical honesty what we are, to repent of this sorry state, and to launch out and grasp Jesus Christ. At this moment, I see very little of this radical honesty, and little willingness to repent of what our churches are. Until we can take this first step, it is unnecessary to speak of further steps toward renewal (from *The God-Evaders*).

11

"YOU MAY ALL PROPHESY ONE BY ONE" (1 COR. 14:31)

The Lord's purpose in the history of redemption was to move from a restricted priesthood to a priesthood of all believers under Christ. This new reality was prophesied in Numbers 11:24-29.

> So Moses went out and told the people what God had said. He called together seventy of the leaders and had them stand around the Tent. God came down in a cloud and spoke to Moses and took some of the Spirit that was on him and put it on the seventy leaders. When the Spirit rested on them they prophesied. But they didn't continue; it was a onetime event. Meanwhile two men, Eldad and Medad, had stayed in the camp. They were listed as leaders but they didn't leave camp to go to the Tent. Still, the Spirit also rested on them and they prophesied in the camp. A young man ran and told Moses, "Eldad and Medad are prophesying in the camp!" Joshua son of Nun, who had been Moses' right-hand man since his youth, said, "Moses, master! Stop them!" But Moses said, "Are you jealous for me? Would that all God's people were prophets. Would that God would put his Spirit on all of them."

This began to be fulfilled on the Day of Pentecost when Peter cited the prophet Joel, "It shall come to pass in the last days, says God, I will pour out my Spirit on all flesh, and your sons and daughters will prophesy, and your young men shall see visions, and your old men shall dream dreams; and on my servants and handmaidens I will pour out my Spirit and they shall prophesy"

(Acts 2:17-18). When Jesus came in the Spirit on Pentecost, all of the Lord's people could now pray and prophesy for the building up of others. We see this then unfolding in 1 Cor. 14 where Paul says, "each one of you has a song, a teaching . . ." and "you may all prophesy one by one."

By 300 A.D. this one-another gathering was soured by the ascension of leaders who eliminated the freedom of the saints to express Christ. The wells of living water were filled by the bodies of leaders who blocked the flow. It is time for leaders to climb out of the wells and let Christ flow once again.

When all people have been used to is traditional church services, it will be a great challenge for those who have been in pulpits and pews to have the Spirit guide them into open gatherings where Christ as dead and raised is all in all. But the blessings of seeking Him as Leader are untold.

A beautiful song, "Make Room," says in part, "Shake up the ground of all my traditions, break down the walls of all my religion; Your way is better, Your way is better."

12

"DO YA THINK?"
By Tim Buss

[Sadly, massive resources over the years have been expended to keep all the religious machinery going, and much of what it does creates endless busyness, a tangle of bureaucracy, and meaningless paperwork, not kingdom advancement. JZ]

D o ya think . . . that the Lord created all the wonders of over 300 billion known galaxies with upwards of three hundred billion stars in each of them and this wondrous planet to sustain life, in order that we might sit in rows and stare at the back of someone's head for an hour every week, while one guy pontificates his narrow and limited view of the eternal Christ, week after week, month after month, year after year, and decade after decade?

Do ya think . . . that You survived the gauntlet of the uterine ascent amongst a bazillion other sperm in order to impregnate an egg and then grow into a multi-billion celled creature just to be reduced to a numbed butt in a pew for an hour a week in the pursuit of knowing Him?

Do ya think . . . that the Son of the living God was born of a virgin, was killed by evil forces, was resurrected by the hand of the Father, was received into heaven, and has sent His Spirit to fill you with the living Christ, just so that you might speak in "thees and thous" in order to communicate with the very living Christ who indwells you?

Do ya think . . . that He has provided a planet large enough to sustain an atmosphere dense enough for us to breathe in and metabolize billions of oxygen atoms every few seconds sustaining our life from one moment to the next, in order that we should have to dress a certain way to fellowship with Him on Sunday?

Do ya think . . . that He has created the 60 second minute, the 3600 second hour, the 86,400 second day, and the 604,800 second week to make you patiently wait for some hierarchically structured and controlled meeting synthesized by the hand of a man to statically reveal Christ to you?

Or . . .

Are you, with each and every unfolding second of each new day, every micro moment, pursuing and exploring, in ever increasing measure: the height and the depth, the length and the breadth of our wonderful Christ with brothers and sisters who have the very life of our magnificent Creator within them? (From 3rdRace.org)

13

DO WE NEED A MILLION DOLLAR BUILDING?

October 17, 2019

Dear Leadership of ———,

Our family moved to the St Croix Valley in 1983. I've seen a lot of religious water go under the bridge. I believe that the church continues the ministry of Christ on earth. Jesus is concerned about what goes on in churches, as is evidenced by His evaluations of seven assemblies in Revelation 2-3.

In light of Jesus' heart for His bride, when I was recently made aware of a million dollar plus building program at ———, my spirit was deeply grieved. While the motives are noble, are there not perhaps grounds to ask if this is the best use of the Lord's resources in light of the New Testament and our local/national cultural circumstances?

In 1975 Howard Snyder wrote a ground-breaking book, *The Problem of Wineskins: Church Structure in a Technological Age*. I read this book in 1977 and it challenged me to the core. The perspectives he gave are reason to give us pause as to the wisdom of pouring money into church buildings. What is your response to his words?

"What would a denomination do that really wanted to become a church with a New Testament dynamic? Let us suppose . . . First, all church buildings are sold. The money is given (literally) to the poor." (p. 23)

"Dietrich Bonhoeffer wrote thirty years ago, 'The Church is the Church only when it exists for others. To make a start, it should give away all its property to those in need.'" (p. 24)

"With the birth of the church the need for an actual tabernacle or temple passed away . . . All that was necessary was a place to meet together as the Christian community. The most logical place was the home." (p. 65)

"Theologically, church buildings are superfluous . . . . It is hard to find biblical support for constructing church buildings . . . The early church did not build church buildings." (pp. 66-67)

"If you had asked in the First Century, 'Where is the church?' you would have been directed to a group of worshiping people in a house . . . In other words, the church grew fastest when it did not have the help—or hindrance—of church buildings." (p. 69)

"Should we simply abandon the use of church buildings? For many churches, this would be the best solution . . . Remember, during its most vital 150 years, the Christian church never even heard of church buildings. In those days it was mobile, flexible, friendly, humble, inclusive—and growing like mad! . . . Why continue building temples? Why not simply do away with them? Traditional church buildings are unnecessary in an urban world and are often a hindrance to biblical Christianity." (p. 73)

"[There is no reason to] spend hundreds of thousands of dollars to provide a large sanctuary that is used only five or six hours weekly." (p. 74)

"*The Body Church*. This type is closest to the NT experience. It holds no property and needs none. It arranges its worship gatherings according to available space in homes, schools, rented halls or other facilities. Its structure is largely organic, based on a network of small groups bound together by large-group corporate worship experiences . . . Its structure is seen as normal, not provisional or transitional. No plans need to be made for a building." (pp. 75-76)

"A return to faithfulness . . . must mean a return to the profound simplicity of the New Testament." (p. 58)

Clyde Reid, in his 1966 book, *The God-Evaders*, observed, "one of the obvious forms of our religious evasion is the extent to which we invest our energy and treasure in lavish religious buildings, used primarily for an hour a week on Sunday morning . . . Spending hundreds of thousands of dollars on statues, stones, carpets and organs in these crucial times is immoral! It is certainly alien to the spirit of Christ that pervades the NT, for Christ was concerned, not with religious paraphernalia, but with true faith . . . We shudder to think of the mission of Christ being bound to a building requiring monstrous upkeep. There comes a time when the Church, like Christ himself, must be willing to give up its life in order to find it . . . The church building boom in America, which has now reached a billion dollars a year [in 2014 it was 3 billion], may constitute a massive evasion, rather than a sign of growth."

Does it seem like a wise path to invest a massive amount of funds into physical church structures at this time in our history? The financial situation in our country is hanging by a thread. It looks like a time for caution and frugality, rather than an occasion for expending a huge amount of money on brick and mortar.

The area we live in is filled with need. It has virtually no emergency housing for the homeless or abused. You know the needs better than I do. It seems like pouring money into the human need around us would be more in line with Jesus' heart. You have been doing this very well, but somehow a massive, costly building project seems misdirected.

Groups are free to pursue the paths they choose, but I believe there are solid reasons to step back and re-think a million dollar plus building program. Somehow, it just seems out of sync with Kingdom priorities, our place in history right now, and the needs of our community.

Thank you for bringing these thoughts before the Lord and seeking His mind!

Jon Zens

14

THE DRAMATIC LACK OF ATTENTION TO LEADERSHIP IN THE NEW TESTAMENT

By Frank Viola

(Excerpts from *Reimagining Church*, David C. Cook, 2008, pp. 181-185)

Paul's letters make a lot of noise about exemplary action. And they show no interest in titles or official position. Consider this: Every time Paul wrote to a church in crisis, he always addressed the church itself rather than the elders. This is consistent from Paul's first letter to his last. Let me repeat that. Every time Paul wrote a letter to a church, he addressed the whole church. He never addressed the elders.

More striking, every church that Paul wrote to in the New Testament was in a crisis. (The exception was the recipients of the Ephesian letter.) Yet Paul never appeals to or singles out the elders in any of them.

Take for instance Corinth, the most troubled church mentioned in the New Testament. Throughout the entire Corinthian correspondence, Paul never appeals to the elders. He never chastises them. He never commends obedience to them. In fact, he doesn't even mention them. Instead, Paul appeals to the whole church. He shows that it's the church's responsibility to deal with its own self-inflicted wounds. Paul charges and implores the "brethren" more than thirty times in 1 Corinthians. And he writes as if no leaders exist. This is also true for all his other letters to churches in crisis. If church leaders did exist in Corinth, surely Paul would have addressed them to solve its woes. But he never does. At the end of the letter, Paul tells the Corinthians to subject themselves to the self-giving Stephanas and his household. But he widens this group to others, saying, "And to everyone who does likewise."

Notice that Paul's stress is on function, not position. His instruction is placed upon the shoulders of the whole church. The entire book of Corinthians is a plea to the whole assembly to handle its own problems. Probably the most acute example of the absence of leaders in Corinth is found in 1 Corinthians 5. There Paul summons the whole church to discipline a fallen member by handing him over to Satan (1 Cor. 5:1ff.). Paul's exhortation clearly runs against the grain of current understanding. In today's thinking, only those possessing "ecclesiastical clout" are regarded as qualified for such weighty tasks. The difference in the way Paul thinks of elders and the way most modern churches think of them could hardly be more striking. Paul doesn't utter a whisper about elders in any of his nine letters to the churches. This includes his ultra-corrective treatise to the Galatians. Instead, Paul persistently entreats the "brethren" to action.

In his last letter to a church, Paul finally mentions the overseers in his opening greeting. But he does so in a fleeting way. In addition, he greets the overseers only after he greets the whole church. His letter opens with: "Paul and Timothy, servants of Christ Jesus, To all the saints in Christ Jesus at Philippi, together with the overseers and deacons" (Phil. 1:1). This is a rather strange order if Paul held to the importance of church leaders. Following this greeting, Paul talks to the church about its present problems. And he never again mentions the overseers.

This trend is highlighted in the book of Hebrews. Throughout the entire epistle, the writer addresses the entire church. Only at the very end of the letter does he offhandedly ask the believers to greet their overseers (Heb. 13:24).

In sum, the deafening lack of attention that Paul gives to elders demonstrates that he rejected the idea that certain people in the church possessed formal rights over others. It also underscores the fact that Paul didn't believe in church officers the way that we do.

Peter's letters make similar noise. Like Paul, Peter writes his letters to the churches—never to their leaders. He also gives minimal airtime to elders.

When he does, he warns them against adopting the spirit of the Gentiles. In fact, he makes the specific point that the elders are among the flock, not lords over it (1 Peter 5.1–2). The elders, says Peter, are not to "lord it over [*katakurieuo*] the people"(1 Peter 5:3, NLT). Interestingly, Peter uses the same word that Jesus used in His discussion on authority in Matthew. The Lord's exact words were, "You know that the rulers in this world lord it over [*katakurieuo*] their people . . . But among you it will not be so" (Matt. 20:25–26, NLT).

This same emphasis is found in the book of Acts. There Luke tells the story of how Paul exhorted the Ephesian elders to "be on guard for yourselves and for all the flock, among which the Holy Spirit has made you overseers" (Acts 20:28, NASB). Notice that the elders are "among," not "over," the flock.

James, John, and Jude write in the same strain. They address their letters to churches and not to overseers. In fact, they all have very little to say about oversight. And they have nothing to say about official eldership. It's quite clear, then. The New Testament consistently rejects the notion of ecclesiastical officers in the church. It also greatly downplays the role of elders.

15
WHAT HAPPENS IN A 1 COR. 14 STYLE MEETING?

A friend in VA recently asked me in a text, "What happens in a 1 Cor. 14 style gathering?" This was my reply:

Roy, the point is such meetings directed by the Lord Jesus are not predictable, not in a box. The people present have come with Christ in them, with possible rivers of living water coming out from their innermost being. It is like having a feast with each person bringing some portion of Him to the table. It is like a symphony with each part contributing to the whole, with the Lord Jesus as the Conductor. There should be no long sermons in a Jesus meeting, but rather "each and every one of you has a song, a teaching, a tongue, etc." Jesus said in Matt. 23, "Don't be called 'leaders,'" but the history of church is essentially about people wanting to be leaders with titles. Long sermons came later after body life was buried in hierarchy. The blessings of His life flowing through many parts were traded for weekly sermons coming from one part. Paul said, "each one of you has," but tradition contradicts and says, "be ears in pews to hear a mouth in the pulpit."

— Jan 16, 2023

16

OVERCOMING FEARS THAT ACCOMPANY A NEW PARADIGM

[These are excerpts from Jon's *The Pastor Has No Clothes: Moving from Clergy-Centered Church to Christ-Centered Ekklesia*]

A great deal of reluctance to enter into a new way of being *ekklesia* has to do with *fear*. It's new. It's different. It isn't what most people have experienced as church meetings with leaders up front. They have never seen the practice of simplicity in Christ as it came to expression in the first century. People are almost always afraid of change.

We are afraid of doing church without a human leader. Except, the truth is, we do have a Leader—*Jesus Christ*. Further, the practical reality is that every group will have leadership each time they get together. His Spirit always leads the saints to express Christ one to another in diverse ways, not in a traditional, concrete *pro forma* format. One sister may share something that becomes the theme that others build on—in one meeting or in several; other themes appear in the days, months, and years ahead. Another time, a brother may tell how the Lord ministered to him in the past week, and that leads to different things, which go on from there. The point is, in organic meetings *His Spirit leadership is gracious, fluid, and over a period of time involves everyone.* If a group looks to the same person time after time to get and to keep things rolling by solely providing the essential content of the gathering, then the *living Christ blossoming through all the parts* is soured.

Sadly, in this way I am convinced that we are all like Israel—*we want a visible king*. Read 1 Samuel 8 and see how Israel was not satisfied with having *the invisible God* as their Leader; they wanted to be *like the nations around them* who had visible human kings. It underscores human desire of having someone else tell us what vision to follow, where to meet, what to do, and what to believe—in short, to spoon-feed us like children—thus, we *reject the Lord's leadership*, substituting a vastly inferior system in his place.

We all will have a king. The crucial question is, will our king be *visible* or *Invisible*? Will we run church like the corporations in the world—in other words, be like the world—or will we seek higher satisfaction in *following the One, whom having not seen, we love*?

Do not be mistaken! These behaviors are not limited to the traditional "church" experience. I have seen this phenomenon kill the life expression in simple gatherings just as frequently. Many groups are ruined by the invasion of pastor-wannabes, elder-wannabes and former church officials who claim a false non-scriptural basis to "improve" their gatherings. Even among those who have completely left the institutional church, too often there is a tendency to look for former "leaders" in past settings to provide the impetus for what takes place in the new one.

Those from leadership positions in the institutional church must take their ambitions and history of being "up front" to the cross. They must take their proper place as just another brother or just a sister amongst other brothers and sisters. If not, the group will inevitably revert to an institutional form usurping Jesus' leadership. Simply meeting in a home does not, in any way, ensure that a Christian group functions under Jesus' Lordship. The pressing issue here is whether or not a person or group takes the place of Christ as the center of any fellowship meeting.

We are afraid of trusting the Lord with unknowns. Fear is a natural partner to confronting the unknown. For the believer, however, fear is the outcome of not trusting in Jesus Christ. His perfect love casts out fear. People focus on a human king because they do not trust the King. To come together as believers and not have a bulletin that lists everything that will happen between 11 a.m. and 12 p.m. Sunday morning is rather uncomfortable for most people. Gathering as saints and trusting Jesus by his Spirit to guide every aspect of their time together is truly a wonderful and blessed experience. To come together in a room with other redeemed people and not know exactly what will take place goes against the worldly method of controlling your environment to conquer fear. Every grain of the "natural man" yearns *for a leader to keep us safe within the religious box.* But we *do* have a Leader. We must have faith, allowing for Him to glorify himself through us without the box.

We are afraid to be vulnerable. Truth be told, everything in organic church *grows out of deepening relationships in Christ.* Thus, you cannot have an enriching 1 Corinthians 14 meeting without those attending getting to know each other during the normal course of life apart from the meetings. This, too, challenges us to live other than those "of this world" with a willingness to pursue long-term, deep relationship-building, which only comes from being vulnerable to the observations and interactions of others who are also in Christ, (*cf.* Bill Thrall/Bruce McNicol/John S. Lynch, *TrueFaced: Trusting God & Others with Who We Really Are*, NavPress, 2004, p. 160).

Such vulnerability in the presence of the brothers and sisters only takes place when we feel comfortable in a loving, accepting atmosphere filled with the aroma of Jesus. What a huge chasm between a 1 Corinthians 14 gathering and a typical church service. You can work your way through the elements in a church bulletin with no commitment or love whatsoever to anyone in the pews around you. On the other hand, built in to the lively, engaging meeting of the *ekklesia*—where all are participating—is a Christ-focused caring and interest in others. An open meeting where Jesus is actively being lifted up through many voices is probably not going to feel comfortable to anyone used to being emotionally-disengaged and passively listening to weekly sermons.

There are many fears and unknowns attached to pursuing a new paradigm of *ekklesia*. But the blessings we are missing by not casting ourselves totally on our loving Leader can only be corrected by trusting Him completely to guide our shared life together in Christ.

17

MATTHEW 23:10 – "DO NOT BE CALLED LEADERS, FOR ONE IS YOUR LEADER, CHRIST"

By Jeff Simon

Jeff Simon, Alabama [Dr. Simon was a beloved Pediatrician in his community. Years ago I visited a group Dr. Simon was part of. Sadly, he passed in October, 2021. He sent me this article long ago, and I am submitting it to you now. JZ]

Jesus' view of leadership was vastly different than the views held in the first century, as well as the notions that are held today. Some of Jesus' strongest criticisms were directed at the Pharisees and Sadducees, the religious leaders of that time. Today's church is liberally sprinkled with titles that are found in the New Testament, terms like elder, deacon, pastor, shepherd, overseer, prophet, evangelist. Not only that, other titles have developed over time such as reverend, bishop, and the various ministers (associate, music, and children's) that are in use today. Seminaries, colleges and universities have been set up in order to develop these positions. Bachelors, Masters and Doctorate degrees are often required to hold some of these official positions. Other positions are obtained by appointment (elder, deacon). Some are considered gifts (shepherd, overseer, prophet). Without the success of these leaders, many churches would sink or diminish in size. Good, however, is the enemy of the best, and the question that must be asked is "How does Jesus feel about leadership in the church?"

Interestingly, Jesus was quite clear on His sentiments regarding this issue. Two different dialogs Jesus had sum up His views on church leadership:

> Matthew 23:8-12 — *But do not be called Rabbi; for One is your Teacher, and you are all brothers and sisters. Do not call anyone on earth your father; for One is your Father, He who is in heaven. Do not be called leaders; for One is your Leader, that is, Christ. But the greatest among you shall be your servant. Whoever exalts himself shall be humbled; and whoever humbles himself shall be exalted.*

> Mark 10: 42-45 — *You know that those who are recognized as rulers of the Gentiles lord it over them; and their great men exercise authority over them. But it is not this way among you, but whoever wishes to become great among you shall be your servant; and whoever wishes to be first among you shall be slave of all. For even the Son of Man did not come to be served, but to serve, and to give His life a ransom for many.*

It is from these two passages that any concept of leadership needs to be developed. Every New Testament passage regarding leadership will be flavored by servanthood when viewed through the lens that Jesus established. Firstly, there is no position of pastor or a priest in the New Testament. The term 'pastors' is used only once in the Bible, Ephesians 4:11, and it is plural. It is impossible to build the modern office of pastor from this simple reference. A better definition for the word pastors is 'shepherds,' or ones who help guide the sheep, a servant. There is no example in the NT of a *single* pastor/elder. The word is always *plural*, except when it refers to Jesus as our 'Shepherd.' The New Testament does talk about 'priests'; believers are called *"a royal priesthood"*(1 Peter 2:9). This is not a designated office but a function every believer fills; we each have access to the throne of grace, and offer sacrifices.

Many consider apostles to be limited to the original twelve. In fact, Paul often had to refute this contention, defending his ability to act as an apostle. Even today, the role of apostle is often relegated to the original twelve, plus Paul. Interestingly, the exceptions should cancel out the rule. Firstly, there was Judas Iscariot, obviously a poor example of an apostle. Secondly, there was Matthias, who became an apostle by the luck of the draw. Barnabas was called an "apostle." Finally, Paul, a persecutor of Christians, is added to the twelve. Paul never saw being an apostle as connected to an office. He includes the *"gift of apostles"* (Ephesians 4:11, *The Message*) as something that the church at Ephesus possessed. He not only defended his apostleship, but acknowledged others. In Romans 16:7 Paul writes, *"Greet Andronicus and Junia, my fellow Jews who have been in prison with me. They are outstanding among the apostles, and they were in Christ before I was."* Junia was a female. By definition, an apostle is a 'person or thing that is sent out.' As an "office," religious groups set up specific criteria that define who can hold this position. As an act of service, however, the role is open to anyone who is 'sent out.'

An evangelist is also listed in the gifts of Ephesians 4:11. Philip is described as an evangelist in Acts 21:8 as is Timothy in 2 Timothy 4:5. An evangelist is someone who 'announces Good News.' This was a common secular term in the first century that Christians also used. Once again, it is a service and not an office. By the way, Philip's four daughters are described as *prophetesses*.

Elders and deacons are detailed more than the other functions. Luke writes about elders in Acts 14:23 saying, *"Paul and Barnabas appointed elders for them in each church and, with prayer and fasting, committed them to the Lord, in whom they had put their trust."* Utilizing Jesus' concept of leadership indicates that elders are the lowliest of servants. In this context, an elder is a more mature Christian who serves. Interestingly, the terms Paul uses for elders are gender neutral. For instance, Titus 1:6 says *"such a person"* (gender neutral) and continues *"being faithful to their partner"* (gender neutral). This is even more evident as Titus 2 describes how the elder men and elder women are to train up the newer Christians. Also, in Titus 1, Paul equates elders and overseers, indicating that it is more of a function than a title.

More evidence that an elder is one who serves is shown by the fact that elders are not instructed by Paul to fix church problems. In all of his letters to troubled churches, never does Paul ask an elder to take over and lead. He always instructs the brothers and sisters to work out the problem. Why? Because decisions are made by consensus and elders are servants who are merely members of the body of equal standing with the rest of the brethren. There is one Head, who is Christ, and one body, whom we are equal members of, and the body receives its instructions from the Head; no part of the body has authority over another part. Granted, Hebrews 13:7 reads *"Obey your leaders and submit to them, for they keep watch over your souls as those who will give an account."* However, this is a misleading translation. The Greek word for 'obey' is *peitho*, and not *hupakouo*, which is the usual word for "obedience." *Peitho* means to "persuade or win over." For instance, in Acts 18:4, it is said of Paul, *"And he was reasoning in the synagogue every Sabbath and trying to persuade Jews and Greeks."* The same word *peitho* is used here to designate *"persuade."* In essence, Hebrews 13:17 reads, "Allow yourselves to be persuaded by your guides."

[The NIV translation of Heb. 13:17 perpetuates some serious misunderstandings. The Greek verb *peitho* means to persuade, and it is in the middle voice—"let yourselves be persuaded by those . . . " The contextual reason why the author is exhorting the people to be persuaded is because the guides were good examples of holding onto Christ in the New Covenant. There is no basis for the phrase "their authority." As Leon Morris notes, "there is nothing in the Greek to correspond to the NIV's 'their authority'; *hypeikete* means simply 'yield' or 'submit'" (*The Expositor's Bible Commentary*, Vol.12, p. 152). To "let yourself be persuaded" implies discernment, not a blind following of people just because they occupy an alleged "office." These people needed to let themselves be persuaded by these particular guides because they were excellent examples of devotion to Christ, and refused to go back under the beggarly elements of the Law. — JZ]

Being an elder or overseer is available to anyone in the body. Paul writes to Timothy in 1 Timothy 3:1 *"Whoever aspires to be an overseer desires a noble task."* If a person is able to aspire to the task, then it is not a function limited to only a select few, but a position of service achievable by anyone. Once again, gender neutral terminology is utilized. *"Whoever"* is gender neutral as well as *"faithful to their partner"* (verse 2). Because of their examples of service, their guidance of the new believers and their maturity in Christ, a believer is not to be resistant to their opinion, but open minded, allowing themselves to be persuaded by their influence.

The definition of the Greek word *diakonos,* translated "deacon," is "one who renders service to another," or "one who waits on tables," obviously supporting the idea that leaders are servants. Although many Bible translations render this as a function relegated to men, the Greek highlights this role for men and women. After discussing deacons in general, Paul specifically instructs female deacons in 1 Timothy 3:11 saying *"In the same way, the women . . ."* Paul is clearly describing woman deacons in this verse. He then concludes his discussion about deacons with *"Deacons must be faithful to their partner."* This cannot be translated as a *"faithful to their wives"* because, not only is the Greek gender neutral, but this contradicts a woman's ability to be a deaconess. Further proof that Paul endorsed female deacons is found in Romans 16:1 where he writes, *"I commend to you our sister Phoebe, a deacon of the church in Cenchreae."* Clearly, deacons are a function of service open to all.

Jesus' commands regarding leadership are few. Unlike the Gentiles, we are not to exercise authority or lord it over people. We should not use titles like 'Rabbi,' 'father' or 'leader' because the Son is our Teacher and our Leader, and God is our Father. We should treat each other equally because we are all brethren. Paul reiterates these sentiments in Galatians 3:28 where he writes, *"There is neither Jew nor Gentile, neither slave nor free, nor is there male and female, for you are all one in Christ Jesus."* All interpretations of leadership need to be screened through the words of Jesus, whether interpreting a Bible verse or evaluating a practice in the church. Any practice that creates a hierarchy (positional, financial, or by gender) needs to be soundly refuted. Any practice that promotes equality, is focused on Jesus, and allows His Spirit to lead is laudable.

The hierarchal structuring of the modern church cannot be supported by Jesus' words. Jesus' position on leadership was diametrically opposed to the religious order of His time; He did not try to pour a new teaching into their old wineskins. The new wine that he brought had to be placed into something new, something vast that could contain the God of this universe, the wineskin of our spirits. Jesus' new paradigm involved the expression of His body on the earth through the *ekklesia* where He alone is Leader. How is this possible? His desires will be expressed through His body by the Holy Spirit. Jesus tells us in John 14:26 *"But the Helper, the Holy Spirit... will teach you all things."* To create a hierarchal system where the titled few lead, the majority follow, and most decisions are made by a sub-group in the church is counterintuitive to the Head and body model, and plainly contradicts the simple teachings of Jesus. *Ekklesia* leadership is simply servanthood and allowing the Head to have dominion over the body.

EIGHT KEY QUESTIONS THAT NEED ANSWERS

I. We have pretty much built our practice of church around a key person, "the pastor." If you were locked in a room with a New Testament, where would "the pastor" notion jump out of its pages to you?

II. Hearing a sermon from a pastor up front with a seated listening audience is commonplace. Where is the centrality of preaching—the weekly sermon—to be found in the New Testament?

III. Why is the open, participatory meeting portrayed in 1 Corinthians 14 ignored, avoided and not practiced?

IV. Why have we exalted into prominence that for which there is absolutely no New Testament evidence—the pastor and preaching—and buried that for which there is abundant evidence in the NT—58 "one another's" and an open body gathering?

V. Many people feel like they have not been to church unless they hear a sermon. They feel like that because of the falsehood they have been taught. What teaching in the NT would inform your conscience that you need to hear a sermon, when sermons delivered by one person are unknown in the NT?

VI. Leaders have blocked the flow of Christ through all His people since 200AD. When will we wake up and realize that the dominance of one or a few leaders has frustrated the Lord's eternal purpose in Christ? Believers are Jesus' body on earth, and this body through which Christ is expressed, as Paul taught, "is not one part, but many.

VII. We say that "the Bible is our final authority in our faith and practice." Yet it seems like we claim to hear the Bible as it speaks to our *personal* lives, but we give no evidence of caring what He says about our *life with others* in the *ekklesia*. How can we claim to be listening to the Lord in our faith and practice when we focus on one person's ministry, structure everything around a weekly sermon, and deny the relevance of 1 Cor. 14 as to how we gather together? The pastor and the sermon are nowhere to be found in the Bible, yet our assumptions about church are built on these two items. Why does our claim to the Bible's "final authority" fly out the window when it comes to our practice of church?

VIII. On what basis can we claim "revival," "outpouring," and "renewal" when our key, long-standing human traditions nullify the Word of God among us? As Jesus said to the religious leaders of His day, "in vain they worship Me, teaching teachings that are commands of humans; you leave the commandment of God and hold fast to human tradition; you have a fine way of rejecting the commandment of God, in order to keep your tradition; making void the Word of God through your tradition which you received, and many such things you do" (Mark 7:7-13). The pastor, the pulpit and the pews have blocked the expression of Christ through His body for endless years. When are we going to say, "Enough," jettison these toxic traditions, and allow Jesus to freely flow through *ekklesias* where He is welcome? The Lord says, "each one of you has" a contribution, and "you may all prophesy one by one." When are we going to reject destructive traditions of human origin and allow the Groom's words to have free course among His Bride?

"The *ekklesia* is Christ's body, in which He speaks and acts, by which He fills everything with His presence" (Ephesians 1:22-23, *The Message*)

FOR FURTHER REFLECTION

Roland Allen, "Tentmaking," *The Ministry of the Spirit: Selected Writings of Roland Allen*, Eerdmans, 1972, 208pp.

Tim Allston, "Jesus Champions 'Silver Medal' Leadership: Becoming Number One by Embracing Number Two," *Ministry*, March, 2023, pp. 10-12.

Christopher Ash, *Listen Up! A Practical Guide to Listening to Sermons*, The Good Book Co., 2009, 22pp.

Pierre Berton, *The Comfortable Pew*, J.B. Lippincott, 1965.

Ori Brafman and Rod Beckstrom, *The Starfish and the Spider: The Unstoppable Power of Leaderless Organizations*, Portfolio, 2006, 240pp.

Rita N. Brock and Rebecca A. Parker, *Saving Paradise: How Christianity Traded Love of This World for Crucifixion and Empire*, Beacon Press, 2008, 552pp.

Emil Brunner, *The Misunderstanding of the Church*, Lutterworth, 1952.

Neil Cole, *Rising Tides: Finding a Future-Proof Faith in an Age of Exponential Change*, Starling Initiatives, 2018, 200pp.

Claudio and Pamela Consuegra, "My Bucket is Running Over: Cumulative Stress in Ministry," *Ministry*, July, 2018, pp. 10-13.

Jack Deere, *Even in Our Darkness: A Story of Beauty in a Broken Life*, Zondervan, 2018, 283pp.

Philip F. Esler, *Modelling Early Christianity: Social-scientific Studies of the New Testament in Its Context*, Routledge, 1995, 349pp.

Cheryl Forbes, *The Religion of Power*, Zondervan, 1988, 144pp.

Joel Gregory, *Too Great a Temptation: The Seductive Power of America's Super Church*, The Summit Group, 1994.

Herbert Haag, *Clergy & Laity: Did Jesus Want a Two-Tier Church?*, Continuum International Publishing Group, 1998.

Uta Ranke-Heinemann, *Eunuchs for the Kingdom of Heaven: Women, Sexuality and the Catholic Church*, Doubleday, 1990, 368pp.

Ronald Hock, *The Social Context of Paul's Ministry: Tentmaking & Apostleship*, Fortress Press, 1995, 116pp.

"How Many Hats Does Your Pastor Wear?" *Christianity Today*, February 3, 1984, pp. 24-27.

Wes Howard-Brook, *Empire Baptized: How the Church Embraced What Jesus Rejected*, 2nd – 5th Centuries, Orbis Books, 2016, 342pp.

William Howitt, *A Popular History of Priestcraft in All Ages and Nations*, London: Effingham Wilson, 1833; reprinted, 1982, Milton Printing, Milton, Florida, 305pp.

Anne-Quitterie Jozeau, "Controversy in Belgium After Group Demands a 'Church Without Priests,'" LaCroix International, March 13, 2023.

S. Joseph Kidder/Jonny Wesley Moor, "Finding God in Community," *Ministry*, January, 2019, pp. 10-13.

Hans Kung, *The Catholic Church: A Short History*, Modern Library, 2003, 230pp.

Hans Kung, *Why Priests? A Proposal for a New Church Ministry*, Doubleday, 1972, 118pp.

LaCroix International, "Controversy in Belgium After Group Demands a Church Without Priests," March 9, 2023.

Julie Lane-Gay, "Celebrities for Jesus: How Personas, Platforms and Profits Are Hurting the Church," *Crux*, 58:2, 2022, pp. 37-39.

John McInnes, *The New Pilgrims: How 20th Century Christians Can Maintain a Simple, Caring Lifestyle*, Ronald N. Haynes Pub., 1981, 211pp.

Greg Ogden, *Unfinished Business: Returning the Ministry to the People of God*, Zondervan, 2003.

Richard Quebedeaux, *By What Authority? The Rise of Personality Cults in American Christianity*, Harper & Row, 1982.

Milt Rodriguez, *Eyes Wide Open: Seeing the Unseen*, Palmetto Press, 2023, 240pp.

Milt Rodriguez, *The Community Life of God: Seeing the Godhead as the Model for All Relationships*, 2009.

Auguste Sabatier, *The Religions of Authority & the Religion of the Spirit*, London: Williams & Norgate, 1904, 460pp.

Judy Schlinder, "The Rise of One Bishop Rule in the Early Church," *Baptist Reformation Review*, 9:2, 1980.

David Sedlacek and Rene Drumm, "My Well Is Empty," *Ministry*, May, 2023, pp. 12-14.

Shelly Speaks with "Pastor" John About His Sermon Last Sunday, https://www.youtube.com/watch?v=WQ34Nl-XZRQ

Christian Smith, "Doing Church Without Clergy," *Going to the Root: Nine Proposals for Radical Church Renewal*, Herald Press, 1992.

Mark Strom, *Reframing Paul: Conversations on Grace and Community*, InterVarsity Press, 2000, 256pp.

Kim Tan, *Lost Heritage: The Heroic Story of Radical Christianity*, Highland Books, 1996, 272pp.

Frank Viola and George Barna, *Pagan Christianity?*, Tyndale, 2012, 291pp.

Gordon Walker, *Twentieth Century Apostleship*, Conciliar Press, n.d., 17pp.

Marjorie Warkentin, *Ordination: A Biblical-Historical View*, Eerdmans, 1982, 202pp.

Garry Wills, *Papal Sin: Structures of Deceit*, Doubleday, 2001, 326pp.

Garry Wills, *Why Priests? A Failed Tradition*, Penguin Books, 2014, 320pp.

Jon Zens, *58 to 0 – How Christ Leads Through the One-Anothers.*

Jon Zens, *Jesus Is Family: His Life Together.*

Jon Zens, "Pulpit or Participation?" YouTube.

Jon Zens, "The Anabaptists – The Untold Story," https://www.patheos.com /blogs/frankviola/anabaptists/

Jon Zens, *The Pastor Has No Clothes: Moving from Clergy-Centered Church to Christ-Centered Ekklesia.*

Jon Zens, "The Tucson Videos, 2016," YouTube.

For more information about Jon Zens,
or to contact him for speaking engagements,
please write to:
Jon Zens
PO Box 548
St. Croix Falls, WI 54024
715-338-2796; jzens@searchingtogether.org.

Many Voices. One Message.

www.quoir.com

Printed in the USA
CPSIA information can be obtained
at www.ICGtesting.com
CBHW051207181023
1366CB00001BA/1

9 781957 007793